Your Sins Are Forgiven

Your Sins Are Forgiven

Ian Petit OSB

Illustrated by
Elizabeth Ruth Obbard

DARTON · LONGMAN + TODD

First published in 1993 by
Darton, Longman and Todd Ltd
1 Spencer Court
140-142 Wandsworth High Street
London SW18 4JJ

ISBN 0–232–52018–6

A catalogue record for this book is available
from the British Library

Cover: design by Sarah John

Phototypeset by Intype, London
Printed and bound in Great Britain
at the University Press, Cambridge

Contents

Acknowledgements

The Scripture quotations in this publication are from *The Jerusalem Bible* and *The New Jerusalem Bible*, both published and copyright by Darton, Longman and Todd Ltd and Doubleday and Co. Inc. Excerpts from the English translation of *The Roman Missal* are copyright 1973, International Committee on English in the Liturgy, Inc. All rights reserved.

Introduction

This book is not a theological treatise on the sacrament of reconciliation, it is rather what one pilgrim, over many years, has come to understand and has found helpful, after much wrestling and searching. My insights are my insights, I trust they are also the Church's, and I offer them in simple language. In doing so, I know I run the risk of being misunderstood. I prefer to do this, though, rather than have everything so doctrinally perfect that the ordinary person cannot understand it.

At one time confession (now called the sacrament of reconciliation) was a regular occurrence in the life of most Catholics; but since Vatican II it has become far less frequent for many, and for others has altogether ceased.

There are many reasons for this. I feel one of the main ones is the failure to relate the sacrament to the redemption already won by the Lord. Perhaps too much emphasis has been put on sacraments and not enough on the Lord who touches us through them.

I, certainly, misunderstood the Catholic teachings that I received and it was only through a crisis of faith that I discovered what being a Catholic really meant. Through counselling many people, I have discovered that my misunderstandings are quite common. I have therefore written this book in the hope that one man's struggles, questionings and ponderings, might be of some help to others.

In confession one meets very complex problems to which there often seem no legitimate solutions, and a priest is faced with both exercising the mercy of God and seeing that sanctions are not given to a state of living which is forbidden by God. I confess I shall not be dealing with such complex problems in this book; rather my reason for writing is to help very ordinary people find, or refind, the extra-ordinary power of this sacrament, not just to forgive sins, but also to free us from them.

1

Misunderstandings

 Truths are not just for learning, we have to dare to live them and thus discover that they are true. This is a risky business because they may be found wanting. Our temptation is to keep them as truths known but untried. Who can describe the utter panic one experiences when the rock on which one stands suddenly appears to be made of sand.

We have all got our stories, mine is one among millions, neither better nor worse. I have no real answers, and I am beginning to realise that knowing answers is not that important. What is important is that I am asked to believe that I am loved beyond measure and have been bought at a terrible price. All my training to be successful, to master my life, cries out against such a truth, because popular belief teaches that we are valued by what we do and not by what we are. In thinking, we try to master situations, for we imagine that when we know, then we are in control. How difficult it is to surrender, yet surrendering will be the greatest thing we ever do.

There is no guarantee, even if the truth has been well taught, that it will have been learnt correctly. Communication is not that simple. People hear what they hear, and they will put their own interpretation on it. I am still amazed, even alarmed, at my own misunderstandings of what I was taught. I do not accuse any of my teachers of teaching me wrongly. I heard what they said, but I coloured it with what was already in my mind. I could even answer correctly the questions put to me, but I now see that those answers were not my answers, I was only giving back what I had heard. I have often said that I would like to have repeated my theology several years after I had been ordained a priest – then I would have had real questions needing real answers.

It was only at a time of crisis that I discovered that many of the truths that I had learnt from others were, in fact, just other people's answers, and they had not become my answers. In other words I was living on what others had said and was now questioning whether I really believed the answers I had been given. It was not that I disbelieved them, I had only accepted them intellectually and did not actively live by them. I do not think there is anything very shocking in that. The trouble is that truth can often remain as something learnt and does not become something believed in.

As a priest I have counselled many people and I have found immense ignorance with regard to the basic message of the gospel. My experience was the same, so I am not surprised at it. It is quite understandable for often when we were being taught these truths, religion was not our most popular subject, and from a career point of view, it was not the most important. Bits of information were picked up and the final picture often bore little resemblance to the truth.

To illustrate what I mean, imagine someone who has never seen anyone play golf. Perhaps his first reaction at seeing someone hit a ball, would be one of marvel and amazement that such a small ball could be hit with such an odd-looking instrument. What skill, he would think to himself! He may even be tempted to have a go, and so he buys a club and some balls. His first attempts are disastrous: try as he might he cannot manage to hit the ball. Finally he buys a book and slowly learns about keeping one's eye on the ball, how to hold the club, how to stand. In time he becomes quite proficient and is able to hit the ball a fair distance in the right direction. But he cannot be called a golfer, because he has not yet learnt the point of hitting the ball – no one has told him that he has to get the ball into the hole in the least number of shots. It is true that he has become quite expert at part of the game. The same can happen with the gospel – we can become quite proficient at part of the gospel, but if we have never learnt its heart, then we only know part of the message. In order to understand the Church and its practices and ceremonies, we need to know and understand the mission of Jesus Christ.

I wonder if, after the Reformation, priests and teachers of the Catholic faith reacted to what the Protestants were protesting about, and began putting a strong emphasis on some of those very doctrines that caused dissension, with the result that the Eucharist, confession, Mary and purgatory received special attention. Over a long period of time this could produce people who were more steeped in Catholic doctrine than they were in basic Christian beliefs. Nothing has actually been denied, it just means not enough has been taught.

I was in that boat – I knew part of the gospel but the very core was missing. It is not surprising if any who have had the same experience do not understand the Church's practices; they lack a true understanding of the mission of Jesus Christ.

As I grew up 'grace' was something I heard much about. In many ways it is not a good word because it is a neuter and grace becomes thought of as an 'it'. True, it does mean 'gift', but to a young child that is not obvious. I thought of grace as being like spiritual petrol enabling me to do good things, and it was always wise to make sure your tank was fairly full of it, just in case death should intervene. Sin, rather like dirt in a petrol tank, stopped grace from acting efficiently – though I confess I was not too sure how all that worked. What was clear was that the sacrament of confession was important because, in some way, it removed the bad effects of sin and gave me more grace.

Grace was significant and it seemed that I had to get as much of it as I could. With this emphasis on 'grace', I can now see that I came to imagine that 'grace' would save me and so I had to try and acquire as much as possible. My mind was locked into this idea and everything was coloured by it. What a crisis I went through when I began to see that it was Jesus who saved and not grace. I felt very akin to Luther and really understood for the first time what 'salvation by faith' meant. I was suddenly faced with the question, 'Was the Church of Rome right or wrong?'

I am not someone who makes quick decisions so I did not go rushing out of the Church. I did spend some miserable years trying to sort myself and the Church out. Was I too Catholic in my upbringing? How could I have missed the gospel message? Slowly, gradually and painfully my mind began to clear and I could see I had laid too much stress on grace and sacraments instead of on the Lord. How important it was that I went through that crisis for I can now see the riches of the Church with clearer eyes. I see the sacraments as very much part of the Lord's plan, but I can also see that if we are not taught carefully what the Lord did for us, then sacraments can become substitutes for God.

I have counselled enough people to know that my experience is not unique and it was this that prompted me to write the book *This is My Body* in which I showed that the Mass continues in us the work that Christ has already completed on Calvary. I see sacraments as making present in us what the Lord has already done. Many people have dropped going to confession. Once it was greatly used, maybe over-used, but what a loss it is not to see how great a gift is offered us. I hope my thoughts, my mistakes and my misunderstandings may help some to re-find this gift that God has given to us.

2

Sin – What Is It?

 We may wonder how these mis-understandings happen. There are several reasons, some natural, others spiritual. To pass a truth on to another person is not that simple. Each of us is individual and through a whole series of events and circumstances we pick up impressions and feelings, and we interpret what we hear according to what life has taught us. Words, meaning one thing for the speaker, may evoke something very different for the listener and this is bound to colour the way in which they are heard.

What is more important, and in spite of opinions held today we must not forget it, is that there is a deceiver, Satan – known as the father of lies. We can be sure that he is very anxious that we do not hear the truth, or, if we do hear it, that we will misunderstand it, for it would be a very real threat to his kingdom if we became convinced of the truth.

There is a battle going on for our mind. Whatever gets into our mind is either filed away in the memory or is acted upon. There is an evil power anxious to fill our minds with untruth.

We were made by God and for God (Col. 1:16). This means that our complete fulfilment will be found in living and existing totally for God. Free will is not the liberty to do what we want, it is the liberty to do willingly what we were made for. So for us humans, the peak of our contentment is willingly existing for God.

In the Fall, through a series of subtle deceptions, Adam and Eve freely chose not to live for God, but to live for themselves, making their own decisions as to what is good or evil. Today much time and energy is spent in arguing about exactly what happened at the Fall, and all this seems to do is to keep us from admitting the fact of the Fall itself and from acknowledging the nature of original sin.

Quite starkly, sin is our refusal to admit that God is God and that we are his creatures; it is our bid for independence, our bid to say we are God, not just made in his image. It is a deep rebellion of the creature against the Creator; a refusal to serve or obey. When God is made to appear as a rival, then he appears demanding, threatening, out-there, against us, opposite, and we fear him. We become suspicious of his promises, and these now appear as punishments or threats, and he who is all good is not trusted by us for he seems to our distorted vision to be dangerous.

What a distortion of the truth this is! When we speak of a 'darkened mind' this is what we mean: God who is all good appears to us as a threat. Many, many people see God in these terms. Usually they will not admit to such thoughts, and so these thoughts have gone into the unconscious and may only surface at a time of crisis. But how is it that God is seen in such a way? We need to remember that there is an enemy within, a fifth columnist, who plays on our fallen nature whispering untruths to us, appealing to our desire for freedom, liberty and self-expression.

We did not become sinners the day we committed our first sin; we were born sinners. It is not by sinning that we become sinners; we sin because we *are* sinners. This truth is clearly taught by the Church and by Scripture, yet how few people really know it. Today, there is a move to talk about 'original blessings' rather than 'original sin' – another example of our rebellion against the truth. In history there have been those who have ranted and raged giving us the impression that human nature is sin-soaked, and it may be in reaction to this sort of thinking that we now prefer to talk of blessings. Original sin is a fact, but that does not mean that sin is intrinsic to human nature. The incarnation is proof of that. Let there be no mistake, if we play down original sin, we play down the need for redemption.

God's plan was that we should be in his Son. He planned this from all eternity. 'Before the world was made, he chose us, chose us in Christ, to be holy and spotless . . . for his own kind purposes' (Eph. 1:4–5). The Fall was not in his plan; the Fall came about through our free will. But God's plan has not changed; rather, he has had to take the Fall into account. In this sense we can talk about the 'original blessing', which is still God's plan, but to harp back

to that, ignoring that there was a Fall, is a failure to
see things as they are.

Sin blinds us

Jesus told us that his Spirit would show the world
how wrong it is about sin. If you ask people what
they think sin is, you will see how right Jesus was.
You will hear many different opinions and I imagine
hardly anyone will say that sin is our refusal to
admit that God is God, our refusal to believe in him
and in what he has done through his Son's death
and resurrection.

I know a priest who asked someone, confined to
their home through sickness, if they would like to
go to confession and he was told: 'But, father, I
never go out of the house.' Sin for that person was
something that happened outside, in the street or
somewhere but not at home.

I once upset two ladies by saying in a talk that
death was the penalty for sin. They came to me
at the end of the talk feeling quite hurt over this
statement. In the course of talking it came out that
their brother had died two months previously and
'he was no sinner. Why, he hever harmed any-
body.' Sin for them was something public involving
scandal, physical harm or harm to someone's prop-
erty.

If we are going to profit from looking at the sacrament where sin is both forgiven and taken away,
then it is important that we try to grasp what sin
really is. This is difficult because sin makes us less
and less aware of spiritual realities. It is like a drug,
it dulls our perception of the truth. Kierkegaard

once said: 'To have a weak understanding of sin is part of our being a sinner.' If you want advice about a colour scheme, it is best not to ask someone who is colour blind. Or if you want advice about a certain recording machine, do not ask someone who is tone-deaf. So, if we want to know about sin, do not ask a sinner. Only God can tell us what sin is.

Sin hides itself

Psalm 35 (36) says: 'Sin speaks to the sinner in the depth of his heart' – dulling his awareness of the real situation – 'he flatters himself in his mind that he knows not his guilt.' How important for Satan that we do not know our real sin. The very fact that so many are quite unaware of the sin in their lives, shows how the devil really has a trump card in making us so dull-witted with regard to it. Obviously, none of us is so foolish as to say that we are without sin, but we fondly think that we are all right. After all, we go to church, we live respectable lives, we are nice and we really harm no one.

I once heard a retreat-giver read 1 Corinthians 13, substituting the word 'gentleman' for the word 'love': 'A gentleman is always patient and kind; a gentleman is never jealous; a gentleman is not boastful or conceited . . .' The implication clearly was that Christianity is about decency and good manners.

Our originating sin has warped us and we want to live for ourselves. Long before any actual sin gets committed there is a rebellious disposition within us. We are all impregnated with the attitude 'I will not serve'.

17

Sins of injustice

Today sin is often seen as offences against human-kind and there is a tremendous awareness of the terrible injustices being committed all over the world. With the rapid progress of communication, we are able to see in our homes, through television, whatever has happened in the world. Visual communication is very powerful and how marvellous to see historic occasions taking place before our own eyes, or to get caught up in tension-filled moments as we watch teams battling for victory in some sport. But also many horrific scenes are brought into our living rooms and people are becoming more and more aware of the injustices that are being done. There are now many movements for righting the shameful way that the rich nations of the world have bled the poor ones. It was remarkable how the pop stars were able to raise so much money for the starving in Ethiopia, and I felt encouraged that there was a world-wide act of caring.

We are in an age when people's rights are very much to the fore, and again I cannot but rejoice as I see the concern for justice and fair play becoming so important to large numbers of people. Is the world then becoming more humane?

Humanism, however, must not be seen as the same as Christianity. It is not the same because humanism puts the human being in the centre of the stage, whereas Christianity puts Christ there. While many are asserting their rights or clamouring for the rights of this group or that, we need to ask who is clamouring for the rights of God?

So, in summing up this chapter I state again that

sin is the refusal to let God be God; a refusal to accept our state as creature, and we do this because of our darkened mind. St Paul, in his letter to the Romans, singles out *the* sin as this refusal to acknowledge God as God. It is not denying that God exists, it is rather choosing to ignore him that is so evil. It is the refusal on the part of the creature to be creature. It is the repeat of the human being's original sin: 'I will not serve'.

If God can be moved off the scene, then of course all his rights would disappear also. The original sin of humankind was to refuse to acknowledge God as master.

Abortionists claim that we have a right over life and the life of an unwanted child can be terminated at will. It is no longer what God sees as right, it is what the human sees as right.

I once heard someone say that *the* sin was all the injustices that the first world commits against the third world. While I do not deny the gravity of this sin, or in any way belittle its seriousness by what I now say, I would claim that *the* sin is the failure of Christians to live the heart of the gospel. If we fail to believe really in the power of the Cross of Jesus to save us from sin, then of course we will fall into sins of injustice and thoughtlessness, especially when they can so easily be hidden from our eyes. Trying to right the injustices of this world can end up in another attempt to solve the problems of the world by human power alone and not by what God has already done through Jesus Christ.

If our minds have been so blinded, what are we to do? We need a lamp for our steps and God in his mercy has provided that lamp. He has done an amazing thing and in order to benefit, we need to know what he has done and to accept it by putting our trust in his plan.

3

God's Remedy

 When our vision of God is wrong, we tend to think that it is God who must change and not we ourselves. I doubt, though, if we would own up to thinking that way, because we are masters at deceiving ourselves.

Our eyes are made to function in the light, and so the light is a delight to them. If we damage our eyes, then the light, once a delight, becomes painful to us. It is not the light that has changed, it is our eyes that have changed, and our eyes that need healing.

In the last chapter we saw that we were made *by* God and *for* God and that meant our greatest joy and delight was to live and exist for him. But sin has warped our vision of God, darkening our mind and instead of perceiving him as he really is, he now appears threatening, demanding and someone to fear. It is not that God has changed, it is we who have changed and it is we who are in need of healing.

In St Matthew's Gospel Jesus says that when salt loses its saltiness it is no longer good for anything and it can only be thrown out (5:13). Sin has seriously wounded human nature and to our darkened eyes the all good God appears menacing and threatening. Is it possible to cure the human family of this sickness, or like the unsalty salt, should we be discarded? When cattle get foot-and-mouth disease, they can only be wiped out and a fresh start has to be made. Can the human family, which was made to be God-centred, be cured of the besetting sin of self-centredness? God has come up with a solution which does involve a wiping out and making a fresh start, but the way he does this is wonderful to behold.

God prepares his people

The Old Testament tells the drama of how God constantly woos the people he has chosen as his own. Time and again he has to chastise them, they then repent and he forgives, and this story is repeated over and over again. 'I did forsake you for a brief moment but in great compassion I shall take you back. In a flood of anger, for a moment I hid my face from you' (Isa. 54:7,8).

People worry about the God of the Old Testament who seems to get incredibly angry, but we must remember we are trying to express in human language a God who is beyond our wildest dreams or ideas. It would be terrible if God just did not care what happened to us; the very fact that he reacts to our foolish ways, shows how much he cares. Listen to any parent who is ticking their child off for running out into a road without looking; there will be plenty of anger in their reprimand. The reason for

24

this is they love the child and are angry because the child exposed itself to danger and hurt. Sin harms *us*, not God, and God does not want us damaged by it, hence he reacts.

At times, it does appear as if God is ready to give up his chosen people. We read in Hosea: 'My people are bent on disregarding me; if they are summoned to come up, not one of them makes a move.' Try and imagine what distress that caused God. Yet he cannot bring himself to forsake his chosen ones.

> Ephraim, how could I part with you?
> Israel, how could I give you up?
> How could I make you like Admah
> or treat you like Zeboiim?
> My heart within me is overwhelmed,
> fever grips my inmost being.
> I will not give rein to my fierce anger,
> I will not destroy Ephraim again,
> for I am God, not man,
> the Holy One in your midst,
> and I shall not come to you in anger. (11:7–9)

All the sacrifices of the Old Testament involved an animal being put to death by having its throat cut, causing its blood to flow out and death to follow. The life of the animal is offered in reparation for human sin. The sacrifice was not able to atone for human sin, but it was a gesture and was a foreshadowing of the sacrifice that one day *would* atone for sin.

The life offered on the cross was the sinless, innocent life of the God-man and the laying down of this life was a perfect act of obedience so as to make up for all the disobedience of the human family. Adam's disobedience caused such untold damage, now the obedience of the God-man has healed that wound.

If any wish to benefit from this action of Jesus, they need to be told clearly what Jesus has done for them and they need to accept it willingly by being baptised into Christ.

God's remedy

God's plan to restart the human family without actually wiping out the old race is marvellous in the extreme. He sends his Son, the second person of the Blessed Trinity, to become a member of the human family. Through the overshadowing of the virgin Mary by the Holy Spirit, a child is conceived who is both Son of Man and Son of God. As Son of Man he can legitimately represent the human family; as Son of God, whatever action he does will have immense value because it will be an action done by God.

God's plan is that this beloved Son of his should bear in himself the consequences of all the sins of the human race. Through the incarnation, he has become a member of the human family; through his being baptised by John the Baptist, he has made solidarity with the fallen race, for John's baptism was a baptism of repentance. The innocent Jesus had no need to repent, but he wanted to be baptised into union with sinful men and women and take onto himself their sins.

To have enlightened understanding about the Passion of the Lord and to grasp truly what was

26

going on, we will need much more than human skill or reason. Paul himself tells us that God's way of achieving our salvation appears folly to human reckoning (1 Cor. 1:21). It is the Spirit of God who reveals truths beyond human reason to our spirit (1 Cor. 2:14).

As we have seen, it was through disobedience that our minds have become darkened. God's extraordinary plan is that his Son should become so identified with sinners that he should experience this darkness himself, and yet continue to obey. In 2 Corinthians Paul says: 'God made the sinless one into sin' (5:21). What can that possibly mean? Countless Christians have pondered this text and after many years of wrestling with it I share my limited understanding.

In wanting his Son to stand in for the sins of the human race, the Father was asking something that no mere human could do. No ordinary human being could take on the sins of another, let alone the sins of all the world. But, Jesus is an absolutely unique man; he is both man and God. As God, the Creator, he has a deeper solidarity with the whole human family than any human being could have, and as man he can act in the name of humankind.

The plan of the Father, willingly accepted by Jesus, is for Jesus to experience the separation from God that sin causes. John Saward, in his beautiful book *The March Mysteries*, suggests that when Jesus cried out, 'My God, why have you forsaken me?' he was not giving into despair, rather he was crying out his acceptance of this place of dereliction which he willingly bore in the name of all. Jesus drinks deeply in obedience the bitter cup of separation and experiences the terror of being without the Father. No amount of imagining can plumb the depth of this pain. Beyond the excruciating agony of crucifixion, the Son of God, the closest to the Father, experiences the loss of the Father, and this is all the more painful because it is so undeserved.

At one time, and this shows how our darkened minds work, I thought Jesus was in some way making reparation for us by placating his Father's anger over our sin. I saw him as volunteering to accept the Father's punishment for us. But this puts Jesus and the Father in opposition to each other. Sin does not damage God, it damages us. It is not God who has fallen out with us, it is we who have fallen out with him, and it is we who need healing. Sin has made us disobedient, self-centred creatures. Jesus wishes to step in to where sin has landed us, and willingly to bear these consequences. By that act of obedience he undoes all our acts of disobedience. Adam, the head of the human family, disobeyed while living in a harmonious world; Jesus, the God-man, obeys while living in a world of disharmony.

Far from the idea of Jesus making satisfactory reparation, the Father's plan is one of sheer love. He was willing to allow his own beloved, innocent Son, to be besmirched with our sins and experience the terrible consequences of death and separation, *but* the Father knew the Son, as God, could not be swallowed up by death, and obedient unto the end, he would await the Father's command to rise up out of death. What a cost to both the Father and the Son – both were anxious and willing, even impatient, to accomplish such a plan. 'It was for this very reason that I have come to this hour' (John 12:27).

What love is shown by the Father in surrendering his Son; what love is shown by the Son in exposing himself to such a trial and in commending himself into the hands of his Father who, at that moment, seemed anything but Father. We cannot begin to fathom what it meant for the Son to embrace forsakenness. He endured abandonment for us, standing where the worst sinner would stand and lovingly accepting the consequence of every sin. For love of humankind, God wanted to experience the absence of God – and for him who is the very Word of God, such desolation far exceeds anything that a mortal human being could tolerate or bear. Only God can experience total abandonment. The plan is terrible, but the Son's willing obedience brings healing to the family of the human race.

As with all gifts, two steps are involved: there is a giving and there must be a receiving. We have looked at the giving, now we must turn our attention to the receiving. God has done a very costly thing for us. How tragic, if, through ignorance or a darkened mind, we fail to know the truth and never become set free.

4

How God's Remedy Reaches Us
Through the Church

 What Jesus has achieved needs to be made available to all generations who come after him. God does this by the means of his Church. The Church is Christ, through the Holy Spirit, continuing his work of rescue among us who come after his time here on earth. The Church is to teach God's truth and minister the redeeming work of Jesus.

I suppose all of us have on some occasion wished that we had lived at the time of Christ. Naively we imagine that we would have seen Jesus as we now see him, and therefore think we would have been on his side, forgetting that now we have the benefit of years of history that have shaped our understanding. Jesus would undoubtedly have challenged us just as he challenged the Jews of his time. We, like them, would have been starting from scratch, trying to make out who he was, knowing that he was not one of the official rabbis. This would have meant having to work through a lot of suspicion. His teaching was very challenging and he supported it by extraordinary miracles. I think the experience would have been very unnerving.

The Jews had been carefully taught that there was only one God, and believed the Jewish God was the only God. The surrounding nations believed in many gods and the chosen people were unique in their belief in one God. When Jesus came among them working extraordinary signs, and claiming to be the Son of God, this offended their beliefs and immediately made them suspicious of him.

If I try and imagine myself as one of the crowd listening to Jesus, I can see myself wanting to play it safe and being slow to come out on his side. There was so much against him that there were good reasons for hesitating, yet what he did and said was very challenging. It would have been very tempting to play it safe and leave one's options open. The book of Revelation condemns those who are neither for nor against as being lukewarm, and the Lord did not have very nice things to say about that.

Today, we are faced with a similar challenge, for there are reports of messages and visions seemingly coming from all over the world. How do we react to them? Do we dismiss them as pious talk, waiting for official approval before we accept them; or do we act on them? So living at the time of Jesus would not have made things any easier to accept.

When Jesus ascended into heaven he did not remove his presence from the earth; rather he made it possible for himself constantly to be present everywhere on the earth. Before his resurrection he was confined to the place where his body was. So, in order to hear him speak or have him lay his hands on us, we would have had to find out where he was, and even that was no guarantee that we would be able to get near him, for everyone was wanting to touch him. The chances of seeing him personally would have been practically nil.

Today, Jesus is present in his Church and we do not have to go very far to hear his word or receive his healing touch.

In the last chapter we saw what God was achieving through the death and resurrection of his Son. Jesus died for everyone, therefore his work of salvation must be made available to everyone. Salvation is much more than a passport to heaven; salvation includes being delivered from our self-centredness, being set free to live for others and for the welfare of all on earth. The Church continues this work of Jesus through the power of the Holy Spirit by teaching and ministering the sacraments.

I would be very reluctant to lay down hard and fast rules about how everyone can have the saving work of Jesus applied to them. It is certainly through the activity of the Holy Spirit that the saving work of Jesus is brought to individuals; but once we start judging who is saved and who isn't, then we get into trouble. God is the judge, not us. On the other hand it is for our comfort that we are able to know when God's saving work is affecting us.

Growth of the Church

It is important to understand that the Church has not always been as we see her today. It is strange how we can all but imagine Jesus in Mass vestments, or see the early Church clothed in our modern-day idea of Church. Jesus never told his disciples how to baptise nor how to say Mass. He just said, 'Go, baptise them in the name of the Father and of the Son and of the Holy Spirit' and at the Last Supper he commanded, 'Do this in memory of me'.

It was only gradually as the occasions began to arise that the apostles gathered to make decisions about what the Lord had taught them. Today, many taxing questions have arisen and the Church has to gather and make momentous decisions, interpreting the Lord's mind with the aid of the Holy Spirit. This is no easy task and it was the same for the early Church as it began to deal with problems and developments. One cannot find explicit teaching from the Lord on all seven sacraments, but clearly in interpreting the teaching of the Lord the early Church recognised certain moments when the Lord's saving work needed to be applied to an individual.

Sacraments are visible signs

Sacraments are external, visible signs indicating that the saving work of the Lord is being accomplished within us at that moment. They are for our comfort. We can trust that when certain signs are done, certain words said, and conditions met, then the saving work of Jesus for a specific purpose is applied at that moment.

It is important to know that God is not tied down to sacraments. He is the One who saves and he can dispense his saving grace when he wills and to whom he wills.

Jesus came to forgive sin and take it away

When Jesus began his mission of redemption, he came among a people who had been carefully schooled in the belief there was only one God, and he was Yahweh. He had the immensely difficult task of revealing that he was the Son of God and yet was not another God, and that he was the one who would remove sin by taking it upon himself. He had to unfold this ministry gradually.

The chosen people had a history of frequent lapses into idolatry, and when they were brought to repentance, the external form usually involved the sacrifice of a lamb. The shedding of the lamb's blood was seen as a life being offered in reparation for a life which had gone wrong.

Jesus began his mission with a call to repent and receive the good news of the forgiveness of sins. He then began to unpack who he was and why he had come. When Jesus claimed the power to forgive sins, he met head on the Jewish belief that only God could forgive sin. By demonstrating physical healings, which could be seen and verified, Jesus was leading them to believe that he also had power in the spiritual realm. When the paralytic was lowered through the roof, Jesus said to him: 'Courage, my child, your sins are forgiven' (Matt. 9:2).

The scribes reacted to this, claiming that only God could forgive sins. Jesus replied:

'Which of these is easier: to say, "Your sins are forgiven" or to say, "Get up and walk"? But to prove to you that the Son of man has authority on earth to forgive sins,' – he said to the paralytic

– 'get up, and pick up your bed and go off home'. And the man got up and went home. (9:5–8)

Jesus is the means of forgiveness

Later Jesus began to teach that he was to be the very means by which this forgiveness was to be obtained. 'The Son of Man came not to be served but to serve, and give his life as a ransom for many' (Matt. 20:28). That truth was again brought out at the Last Supper when he said: 'For this is my blood, the blood of the new covenant, shed for many for the forgiveness of sins.'

Jesus hands on the power to forgive

Jesus next began to teach that his disciples were also to hand on this reconciliation (2 Cor. 5:18). First of all he told Peter that what he bound on earth was also bound in heaven and what he loosed on earth was also loosed in heaven (Matt. 16:19). After his resurrection he breathed on his apostles saying: 'Receive the Holy Spirit. For those whose sins you forgive, they are forgiven; for those whose sins you retain, they are retained' (John 20:23).

The power to retain sins indicates that in some way the apostles had to hear what the sins were so that they could judge whether to forgive or retain. The power to forgive was not the power to forgive in their own name but the power to make effective the Lord's redemption in others. 'It is all God's work. It was God who reconciled us to himself through Christ and gave us the work of handing on this reconciliation' (2 Cor. 5:18).

Sins committed after baptism

Jesus never told his apostles exactly how they were to forgive sins, just as God never told Adam and Eve how they were to subdue the world. It seems as though at first the Apostles understood baptism as the way sins were to be forgiven, for the Lord did give them an explicit command to baptise for the forgiveness of sins. Being a Christian was costly, so the first converts were very zealous and devout. But gradually they had to face the problem of those who sinned seriously after their baptism. Matthew, in his Gospel, records Jesus' teaching on a brother who would not receive correction (18:15–18). Paul, in 1 Corinthians 5:1–13, addresses the problem of serious sexual sin and in the Acts of the Apostles we have the story of Ananias and his wife Sapphira deceiving the apostles – so clearly they were encountering the problem of sin after baptism.

We have no record of the sacrament of reconciliation operating until the third century. This does not mean it did not operate – we just have no record of it. It cannot have been easy for the early Church to begin to face the question of sins committed after baptism. Imagine yourself present at one of those meetings. Here we see the Church learning to be Church: learning to trust that it has received the Holy Spirit, but not imagining that this meant instant revelation, but that they needed to meet, pray, recall what the Lord taught and begin to make decisions. This was no easy task. We live at a time when we often imagine that either all the decisions have been made and all we have to do is to see what the Church did in earlier days, or we imagine that we are going to reach decisions by logic and reasoning alone.

Early ways of applying forgiveness

As the Church began to see it had a right to remit sins committed after baptism, this remission was, at first, for serious sins such as murder, apostasy, adultery and others. This remission, they felt, could only be granted once in a lifetime and it was even known as 'second baptism' or 'second penance'.

These sins were to be confessed to the bishop in secret, but the penance was to be performed publicly. Sinners were excluded from the Eucharist, thus demonstrating that sin cuts us off from God. Absolution for sins was not given until after the penance had been performed, for doing the penance was seen as a true sign of repentance. The penitents also had to wear special dress and only hear the Word liturgy at the Eucharist. Because of the practice of public penance this sacrament came to be known as the 'sacrament of penance'. Later, when the penance was no longer practised in public, it was known as 'confession'. As before, absolution for the sins was not given until after the penance had been performed, to ensure true repentance. This absolution was given on Maundy Thursday at a celebration known as 'sacramentum reconciliationis' and after this ceremony the sinners were allowed to take their place in the community again. It was from this ceremony that Vatican II derived the name 'sacrament of reconciliation'.

Changes over the centuries

Because the penances were so severe – strict fasting, the wearing of sackcloth and ashes, kneeling outside the church during services, banishment from taking part in church ceremonies – this sacrament was often postponed until the hour of death. In the fifth century Cassian refers to alternative forms of penance such as acts of charity, almsgiving, acceptance of sufferings, intercession.

It was from St Patrick and his monks that a new form for the sacrament began to appear. The penances were no longer performed in public, though they were still quite severe. More frequent confession was encouraged and to help this, the confession needed no longer be made to the bishop but to any priest. People were encouraged to include less serious sins in the confession, and in time this sacrament was no longer confined to dealing with serious sins. Again, the penances were still quite heavy, including serious fasting, long prayers and pilgrimages to Rome or the Holy Land, and alternative penances were sought. In the twelfth century Abelard attacked the external practice of penance and pointed out that the gospel called for repentance in the heart.

Vatican II changes

Pope John XXIII called for a second Vatican Council to complete the unfinished work of Vatican I, which had to close down because of the Franco-Prussian war. During the Vatican II Council, which undertook to update the Church, the sacrament of forgiveness underwent certain changes. Drawing on the vast information available and world-wide experience, the Church was anxious that this sacrament should find its rightful place in the modern Church. The name was changed from 'confession' to 'reconciliation' to emphasise that it was God's work 'reconciling the world to himself in Christ', whereas 'penance' or 'confession' put the stress on human action.

Also the Church wished that there should be a diversity of ways that the sacrament could be celebrated, and that communal celebration be added to the individual form. The Word of God was recommended, either to be read privately before meeting with the priest, or together with him in the confessional. This was to proclaim the mercy and forgiveness of God, inspiring confidence and hope in the heart of the sinner. Many other changes were suggested and we will be looking at these in a later chapter. But before we consider them we need to look again at God's way of dealing with sin and how forgiveness is brought to each individual.

Need for faith

Sacraments are not magic. We have the word of the Church that they work, whether we feel that they do or not. Sometimes people wonder after receiving a sacrament if it 'worked' for they felt nothing at the time. We must trust in the Church, which teaches that the saving work of Jesus is made applicable to us no matter what we may feel at the time. This does not mean that we just trust in the power of the sacraments and make no effort to prepare and receive them worthily. A row of communicants all receive the Lord, but the effect in each is different according to their disposition. Our eyes must not just be fixed on the sacrament, rather we must focus on the Lord who is touching us through this sacrament.

Faith must be added to sacraments. The sacraments are making effective in us what the Lord has already achieved, so it is very necessary to know what the Lord has achieved and to believe in it.

When Jesus was touched by the woman who had suffered from a haemorrhage for twelve years, she was healed. Many others were touching him at that moment too, but no power went out of him. The reason is that she had faith in him; but note, having faith in him was not enough, she also needed to touch him.

I like to see sacraments as when we approach the Lord and allow him to touch us through his Church. Just as the woman needed to have faith, so too we need to have faith in what the Lord has done for us and ask him to make it effective in us at this moment of touching.

Other ways of reconciliation

Reconciliation is not the only way sins can be remitted. They can be remitted through works of charity or by confessing directly to God. Whenever we acknowledge our sins to God, whether in the confessional or outside, Jesus turns to the Father and says: 'I have dealt with that.' The Spirit of God applies that forgiveness there and then.

If that is so, then why do we need this sacrament?

We need it, first of all, for serious sins, but it is also good to expose our other sins to the power of the sacrament. Also sin is not just between us and God, it is between us and the brothers and sisters in the Church, and God. Just as in the human body, when one member is damaged or has become sick, this will affect the whole body in some way, so also when we live a life of sin, we weaken the body of Christ present in this world and we weaken the spiritual life of the body. We need to ask pardon of the whole body for our offence. By going to the representative of the Church, we are confessing to the whole Church through that representative.

This, of course, does not excuse us from seeking pardon of individuals when we harm them by sin. If we should take away the good name of someone, we need to confess that to God, through the Church's representative, and we also need to make restitution to the individual we have offended and ask for forgiveness.

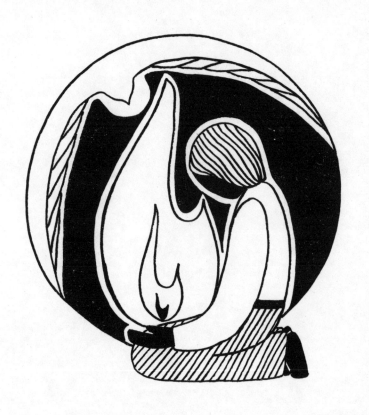

5

Exposing the Right Sins

In the chapter after this one, we will look at the New Rite of Reconciliation step by step, trying to sense the thinking behind the changes, so as to use the sacrament more profitably. Before we do that, some time must be spent in trying to identify our sins and the sin that lies hidden within us. We have seen that sin dulls our spiritual perception, and this can make us very blind to our own sin.

As mentioned already, we did not become sinners the day we committed our first sin; we were born sinners. A sinner is not someone who just commits sins, it is someone in whom sin dwells. Long before sin becomes visible in some action, it is present within us – it is a flaw within, a disposition, a tendency, a proneness towards evil. Jesus did not just come to atone for our committed sins, he came to take away the sin lurking within us.

The blood of animals was incapable of taking sin away, but it was a good illustration that in some way a life had to be laid down in reparation for a life which had gone wrong. The blood of the Son of God was more than capable of atoning for sin; and through the offering of his sinless flesh, sinful flesh was renewed for all who put their faith in him.

In the sacrament of reconciliation two things happen. Our committed sins are forgiven, remitted; and our sin within us is put to death and our new life in Christ is strengthened.

Need to expose the right sins

If the sacrament of reconciliation is to have its two-fold effect, then we need to try and identify the sin within us from which our sinful actions come. Failing to see and confess the inward disposition means we will fail to apply God's remedy for our healing. What is so insidious about sin is that it injects dullness into us; it blinds us, blurs us spiritually, making us unaware of the true situation and because of this we fail to admit the sin so cleverly hidden in us.

What is the sin behind our sin?

If a healing ointment is to be effective, it needs to be applied to the wounded area. In the same way, if this sacrament is to have its healing effect, then we need to know where to let it beam its rays. Where possible we need to confess not just our sinful actions, but also the sinful dispositions that lie behind those acts.

For example, three penitents may all confess to having been unkind. In each case the three sins are

48

very different, yet they are cloaked under the same heading 'being unkind'.

A priest is a shepherd: he is not just curious, he is a pastor and wishes his flock to grow to maturity and full spiritual strength. In asking how the sin of unkindness occurred, he is leading the penitent to better self-understanding. The first penitent has had one of those days when everything went wrong from the very moment she got out of bed. On her arrival home that night, after a very trying day, she found a friend on the doorstep wanting assistance. This was the straw that broke the camel's back, and she blew her stack.

Through talking things over, the priest was able to point out that maybe she was living her life reacting to it by what she felt and failing to remember the Lord's promise to be with her and share her life. The sin she needed to confess was her failure to remember the Lord's promises – a failure to live in that place of peace.

The second penitent was unkind because of jealousy. Someone where he worked was brighter and more efficient, and was also younger, so therefore was a threat to him, causing the penitent consistently to be unkind. Clearly this sin is more serious than that in the previous example because it was very deliberate and was not rising out of frustration or hot-headedness. So the sin that needed to be exposed to the power of the sacrament was jealousy.

The third penitent who confessed to being unkind was someone who was totally absorbed in herself. She felt she was the only pebble on the beach and so it is not surprising she was unkind in her dealings with others. The sin that needed confessing was that of over self-concern.

Sinful attitudes

All this helps us to see it is not only the sins we commit that need to be looked at but we also need to turn our attention to the sin within from where they come. This is not so easy to see and that is why talking things over with another can be very illuminating in uncovering the real sin.

The wound of the Fall manifests its presence in us in different ways. Some people have quick tempers; others are pushy and always trying to be in the centre of everything; others are lustful; others seem to have problems with honesty and are very weak when an opportunity comes to take something that is not theirs. How these faults get attached to differ- ent people, I do not know. Obviously life can give us raw deals, we can get hurt by living and we develop ways of coping. We are also born with different dispositions and these we can name 'orig- inal sin'.

In trying to be conscious of the sin within us, we do not want to become self-probing, doing endless dissections trying to discover our inner sin. We need to ask the Holy Spirit for his illumination, for Jesus told us the Spirit would convict us of sin.

Of course the evil spirit also wants to point out our sin, if he knows we are the type who will give in to guilty feelings and anxiety. When the Holy Spirit points out our sin, he comforts us by remind- ing us that there is a remedy for sin and that is in the Cross of Jesus Christ. So if, when we ask the

Spirit to show us our sins, we find that we become depressed, we should consider whether perhaps the other spirit is at work.

We saw earlier that sin is fundamentally a refusal to acknowledge God as God with absolute right over us. All sin asserts that we are our own master. We may be able to label our sins with names such as lust, jealousy, avarice or some such thing – they all, in fact, stem from the originating sin of rebellion which lies within us. We need to look and see how much of that rebellion is still within us. Just because we go to church, make efforts to practise our faith, we can tend to think of ourselves as good and loyal Christians, and never see the rebellion that is deep within us all. Clear rebellion is fairly obvious to see, but it is the secret rebellion that hides under the guise of religion which is the most subtle.

All sin, fundamentally, is us saying to God that we will go our way and not his. It is good to take an honest look at ourselves and ask, is God first in our lives? Some will be able to admit, straightaway, that he is not. But those who practise Christianity, go to church and endeavour to do what is right, will probably find difficulty in admitting that God may not be first in their life. There is no need to get full of guilt over this, we may well have to admit simply that it is true. It is sad, but it is true. What God wants is that we dare to admit it and ask him to heal us. We cannot ask for healing if we do not think we need it.

If we begin to see how wilful we are, and do not try and hide from that unpleasant truth, then there is a chance that God will begin to do in us what we are unable to do. Very rarely is unbelief confessed, yet it is the most common of sins. We tend to think of it as a sin that belongs to unbelievers. The truth is we just do not believe enough.

Sinful attitudes form us and shape us. For example a self-centred person, constantly putting self first, will meet every situation with the question: 'what is in it for me?' It will not be recognised as selfish. Such phrases from the gospel as 'Come to me all who are heavy burdened' or 'God is close to the broken-hearted' can all be heard willingly and gladly, not because we are God-centred, but because we are self-centred with a darkened mind.

In his teaching 'Blessed are the poor in spirit' (Matt. 5:3) Jesus is saying blessed are you when you discover your spiritual poverty. That discovery is a blessed moment for then the need for God is seen in all its starkness. Such a discovery is gall to self-love, and we can fail to face the hurt and disappointment, and instead immerse ourselves in external activity to prove our worth to ourselves and others.

Jesus came to rescue us from such cloying experiences and often we cannot discover these things by ourselves.

6

The New Rite

Since Vatican II the Church has encouraged a more mature use of the sacrament. For some it had become a bit like a laundromat – you put your list of sins in and out came your absolution. By recommending a room instead of a confessional box, a room where either a face to face meeting or anonymity can be offered, much of the forbidding atmosphere of the dark box has been dispelled. Many have awful memories of this stemming from childhood days, some even have phobias as a result.

The Church also wants to get away from lists of sins and would prefer we dialogued more with the priest. This opportunity to chat with a priest can lead us to a greater self-understanding, bringing us to deeper insights as to where our real sin lies.

So we are encouraged to be less formal or stereotyped in the way we confess, but it is proving quite difficult to break out of the formal ways we have learnt. Confessing our sins is not something we do easily, and it did help a lot to have a set pattern to follow. We asked for a blessing, said how long it was since our last confession, told our sins, received a penance, made our act of contrition, received absolution and left. There was nothing wrong with this, save that it could so easily become a formula with little meaning.

Whenever we go to receive any sacrament we need to remind ourselves of what we are actually about. It is so easy just to 'go to the sacraments'. In the sacrament of reconciliation, we are, in a sense, collecting what Jesus has won for us on Calvary with such terrible cost. Therefore, if we are going to draw the most benefit from this, we need to prepare ourselves.

Let me give an example of how stereotyped we have become. I have often found that, after a chat with someone during which sins have actually been confessed, when I have suggested that they might like to receive absolution, the person has then adopted a strange stance, made the sign of the cross and said: 'Oh bless me, father, for I have sinned' and proceeded to say how long it has been since their last confession. In other words they became quite unnatural. When I pointed out that they had actually already confessed their sins and there was no need to repeat them, they seemed to relax and become normal again.

Preparation

The Church encourages us to read passages from Scripture, especially passages concerned with healing or forgiveness. This is to stir up our faith and trust in God's love. If Jesus, before his death and resurrection, forgave sins and healed people, what can he not do now that he is risen?

Faith is not something we either have or do not have, like beans in a jar; faith is something that must be used, it must be kept active. To believe what Jesus has done, we need to stir up in ourselves confidence that he also came to heal us. Knowing that Jesus came for sinners, gives us fresh heart; therefore reading passages of Scripture which tell about Jesus' love for sinners (Mark 2:15–17; Luke 15:1; Luke 15:11–32) helps us to approach this sacrament with confidence in spite of our sins.

Examen

Remembering what we saw in the last chapter about how sin blinds us and makes us insensitive to its evil, we need to ask the Holy Spirit to enlighten our minds and show us our real sins. If we are not in the habit of reviewing our day each evening, nor in the habit of frequent confession, then this becomes more difficult and it is easy to fall back on lists and numbers.

Admitting our sins and failures is never easy, and people often put little prefixes to their sins. They will say: 'Maybe I have been a little unkind. Maybe I have not lived up to my Christian calling.' All this is understandable, but in fact it is failing to confess honestly. The truth is you either have done these things or you have not. We need to be simple and state what happened. There is no necessity to go into endless details. The honesty of some is most moving.

There are pamphlets or small books that help us

examine our lives. Many find these helpful. I personally find that I can say yes to nearly all the suggestions, and things then get a bit unwieldy.

We all have some sin which is our particular weakness. If we do not know that, then we need to ask the Holy Spirit to show us. Once we know it, we need to look and see why we often fall into that sin. Remember the examples we looked at where unkindness was cloaking several different sins.

While many confessions are edifying, many are woefully unprepared. It can be quite depressing trying to help people look deeper into their lives; you end up wondering if they have any clue as to what it is all about. This is why I have become so convinced about sin blinding us. I have experienced this blindness myself and while most people are not culpable, it is distressing to see how much ignorance exists as to what the gospel is about.

How to begin

The usual way to start is to ask for a blessing, unless the priest has already given one, and then say how long it is since the last confession. This helps the priest for if there are long gaps between each occasion, he may see the wisdom of suggesting a more frequent use of the sacrament. I remember hearing confessions in the West Indies, where I was recuperating after sickness. One small lad started his confession with: 'Bless me, father, for I have sinned. This is my last confession.' I resisted telling him to make sure it was a good one.

The confession of sins

We have spent some time trying to see our real sins, but are any of us able to express those sins in adequate words? Are any of us able to be that honest? I do not think we need to get over-worried about this. I like to think that the words of Jesus, 'Father, forgive them; they know not what they do', are repeated again as we stumble along trying in all honesty to speak in very broken phrases of our sins. Again and again I ponder the saying of St Paul: 'God made the sinless one into sin'. Has Jesus so taken on our sins that in a sense he has already confessed them to the Father? Such a thought as that makes me see the value of confessing to a priest and not just privately to God. When we participate in the sacraments, we are no longer just an individual, we are members of the body of Christ and our actions become his. I remember being taught something about how our imperfect sorrow was made perfect sorrow in this sacrament. For a long time I never really grasped what that meant, but now I think I do see. When we confess directly to God, it is us confessing, but when we confess in the sacrament, then Jesus confesses with us, in us and through us.

What helps me is to know that as I say my sins, Jesus in some way is claiming my sins and telling the Father that he has already dealt with them.

Advice

After we have confessed our sins the priest may want to give some advice or encouragement. At these moments the Holy Spirit can operate in a remarkable way, inspiring the priest to say the right thing, or ask the correct question. Remember, the priest himself has to go to confession and as a penitent-priest he has to admit his sins and failures.

Penance

Normally then the priest gives a penance. We must be clear that it is *not* the performing of the penance that wins the forgiveness of our sins. Our sins have already been forgiven through the death of the Lord, and all we are doing at confession is collecting that forgiveness. As we mention our sins, it is as though Jesus is turning to his Father and saying that he has already dealt with those sins, and he then sends the Holy Spirit to us to apply that forgiveness. If this is so, then why do we get a penance? In the old days one was required to do the penance before one received the absolution. It was a sign of repentance and a mark of a change of heart. Now we receive absolution before we perform the penance. Performing our penance is a sign of our desire to change our ways.

The penance also has something to do with reparation. When someone confesses to stealing, then forgiveness cannot be granted unless the thing stolen is returned. This does not have to be done publicly and if it is impossible to return what was stolen, then some reparation has to be made. When we sin, several people get hurt: firstly God, secondly the Body of Christ, either directly or indirectly, thirdly ourselves. In the sacrament our relationship with God is restored, but the damage we may have caused another is not repaired, nor is the damage done to myself. For example, if I have told lies, I get into the habit of doing that; in confessing the sin, I get pardon but not deliverance from the habit.

I feel there is still work to be done in this area, for the giving of three Hail Marys, or some such penance, often bears no resemblance to the damage caused by our sins. Obviously if unkindness has been confessed, then some sort of reconciliation is suitable. When something has been stolen then restitution has to be made. I feel, where possible, the penance ought to bear some relationship to the confession. On the few occasions when I have tried to be more creative and have given some suitable penance, the penitent has often said at the end of the interview: 'You never gave me a penance, father!'

Act of contrition

There are many forms of acts of contrition, some of which are not ideal for today. I think we need to study the act that we use and see if it really is saying what we would like to say. Many people now make their own acts of sorrow, and these can be very moving.

Absolution

While the priest is giving us the absolution we should listen carefully to the words and deliberately receive them. Now that it is in English and not in Latin, there is no need to make our act of contrition while the priest is saying the absolution. The words sum up most suitably what is actually happening. In a few lines the mystery of Christ's saving death is stated. We need to listen carefully, saying to ourselves, 'So let it be, amen, amen'.

The priest begins the absolution with the beautiful words: 'God, the Father of mercies'. He does not say 'Merciful Father', but the 'Father of mercies'. Then he goes on to state the truth: 'God, the Father of mercies, through the death and resurrection of his Son, has reconciled this world to himself and sent the Holy Spirit among us for the forgiveness of sins'. What sparcity of words and yet how they capture the basic truth. Jesus' death has reconciled us to the Father and the Holy Spirit is now being sent upon the penitent to apply that forgiveness. The priest goes on: 'through the ministry of the Church' – this means you have the guarantee of the whole Church behind this – 'may God give you pardon and peace, and I absolve you from your sins in the name of the Father, and of the Son, and of the Holy Spirit. Amen.' Notice the priest does not say, 'I forgive you your sins', he says, 'I absolve you', that means 'I free you, I loose you from, I break you free'. He often ends by saying, 'Go now, your sins are forgiven.'

I would like to invent a confessional where the priest presses a button at the end of the absolution and trumpets blow. Something stupendous has happened; yet if you stand outside the box and look at the people coming out, you would not imagine that any sin had been forgiven. We need to exercise our faith on what has happened. Too often we judge by our feelings – and that is not the way a Christian should live.

Frequency

It is sad that this sacrament, which was once often practised, has fallen into very rare use by many now. We were encouraged to go frequently and that, under the old understanding of the sacrament, was not wrong. In trying to get a more mature approach, frequency has not been stressed, and there has been more emphasis on the quality of the confession, with the expectation that people would go to confession less often. We are creatures of habit and, if we were once in the habit of going every week or two, it seems much harder to be regular when the period in between is longer. I would not like to regulate just how often a person ought to go, but clearly if the gap between confessions is quite long, then the ability to see accurately what our real sins are will be greatly reduced. People who leave several months between confessions, seem to have difficulty in remembering their sins, and they tend to resort to 'five lies, four impure thoughts, and twenty-seven swear words'. There is little evidence that much thought has gone into such a confession and one wonders how genuine the repentance is.

It takes time for us to change our ways and become familiar with new ones. Confessing our sins is never easy, and finding someone with whom we feel at home, even when face to face, can be a problem. But, remember priests also go to confession, and they also feel the difficulty. But if we keep our eyes on what is actually happening at confession, remembering that what took place with such cost on Calvary is now being applied to us, I think we can learn to cope with the embarrassment.

7

You Have Set Us Free

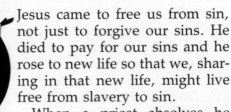Jesus came to free us from sin, not just to forgive our sins. He died to pay for our sins and he rose to new life so that we, sharing in that new life, might live free from slavery to sin.

When a priest absolves he does not say, 'I forgive you your sins', but rather, 'I absolve you from your sins'. Absolving is more than forgiveness, it means breaking free from, a loosening of chains, a healing.

This breaking free, this loosening from sin, is not experienced by many. If anything, the opposite seems to be the norm: sin remains and does not go away. Why is this so? If Satan has been defeated by the Lord through the Cross and resurrection, how is it he still seems to roam about this planet with so much power?

I believe the reason for this is because clear teaching is not given. It is not easy to accept that we are dead in Christ to sin, because we seem anything but dead. Things that are hard to teach often get neglected, and what is not taught does not have faith put in it. To experience the power of Christ's victory, we need to know what that victory is so that we can put our faith in it – for we cannot put our faith in what we do not know.

What is this victory?

The victory – the central theme of the gospel – is that Christ snatched us out of Satan's hands by dying for our sins *and* rose again that we might live in a new way.

We need to unwrap this truth. The laying down of human life that took place on Calvary was more than enough to outweigh all human sins, because that life belonged to the second person of the Trinity. This was God's marvellous plan: human sins should be atoned for by one of the human family who would be capable of obtaining such forgiveness because he was also God. This is celebrated in the Preface III for Sundays in ordinary time: 'You came to our rescue by your power as God, but you wanted us to be saved by one like us.'

But that is not all. Because Jesus is our representative, when he died, all whom he represented also died. We did not die in ourselves, we died *in him*. This is the important truth – *we died in him*.

In order that this death might become a reality in us, we need to accept Christ as our representative. The way we do so is by being baptised into him. We have all been taught that at baptism we were baptised into Christ's death and rose with him that we might live with him in a new way (see Rom. 6:3,4). This truth was demonstrated in the old ritual of baptism when total immersion was practised. The going down into the water represented our dying and descending into the tomb; the rising up represented our being born again into a new life in Christ.

This dying at baptism takes place in the realm of the spirit, not in the realm of the senses or of reason. We have but the first fruits of salvation (Rom. 8:22–4). What takes place in the spirit cannot be felt by the senses, nor really grasped by reason. It is not contrary to reason, just beyond it. It is in this state that we must acknowledge that we live.

The deceiver is still at work

If this doctrine is the very heart of the gospel, then we can be sure that Satan, the father of lies, will do all in his considerable power to obscure it and prevent it from being known. For a very long time I saw the gospel in moralistic terms – be good and you will merit heaven – and I do not believe that I had such a misconception purely by chance. I hadn't really grasped at all that salvation is a *gift* from God the Father through Christ Jesus his Son.

In his general audience on 15 November 1972, Pope Paul VI asked the question, 'What is the greatest need of the Church?' This is how he replied: 'Do not let our answer surprise you as being over simple or even superstitious and unreal: one of the greatest needs is defence from that evil which is called the Devil. Evil is not merely a lack of something, but an effective agent, a living spiritual being, perverted and perverting.'

Knowing a doctrine is not the same as believing in it. If Satan cannot prevent us from hearing the truth, then he is quite content if we let it lie fallow.

We are not dealing in magic here. It is not enough to know the Lord is the Saviour and just to call on his saving power. It is our *faith in* the Lord's saving that releases that power. It is one thing to have been taught that the Lord's death and resurrection saves us, it is quite something else to believe in it and act on it.

God always requires our co-operation with him. He pays us an immense compliment by asking us to work with him. For example, when Christ cured the paralytic, he told him to 'get up and walk'. The Lord did not do that for him; he cured him, and then told him to act on that cure. Again when he sent his apostles out to preach the gospel and heal the sick, they had to obey his word and act on his command. So we, also, have to obey what we hear. Our sins have not only been forgiven, their hold on us has been broken – we have been absolved. We must act on that.

What about will-power?

Often I have asked penitents, after they have confessed their sins, how they plan not to commit those sins again, and I have rarely been given the right answer. The answer usually is, 'I'll try harder, father', and this shows that the penitent still imagines that will-power can conquer sin.

It is not that will-power is not required; the will, however, does not need to determine to make every effort to overcome the fault, but rather to accept God's way of overcoming sin, which is through the death and resurrection of Jesus Christ. 'Lord, by your Cross and resurrection, you have set us free', as we say at Mass. If we are consistently neglecting to use what we say with our lips, then it is not surprising that we do not experience the gospel as power. St Paul tells us, 'I am not ashamed of the Good News: it is the power of God saving all those who have faith' (Rom. 1:16). Satan can make us misunderstand those words and cause us to focus our mind on 'all those who have faith', comforting us that we have faith because we are Catholics. Being in the Church is no guarantee that we believe in the heart of the gospel. We will only experience the power of the gospel when we passionately believe in the death and resurrection of the Lord. Notice, I did not say that we believe *that* it took place; rather we believe in what happened *because* it took place.

Some penitents answer the question, 'How do you plan not to commit those sins again?' by saying that they will pray. Now, while prayer is essential, it all depends on what is meant by prayer. To pray, begging God to set us free, is surely a good thing. It seems so right and correct. But that sort of prayer actually bypasses the essential truth of the gospel – the truth that God *has already acted for our deliverance*.

Ignorance

I fear that much of today's spirituality neglects this central truth and the very heart of the gospel gets left out. I can well remember thinking the gospel was all about being good and trying desperately to practise what Jesus taught. Naturally I prayed for strength to be patient, generous, pure. What is so deceptive is that it all seems right and proper. But to pray to God, as though it was up to us by our prayers to persuade him to act and do something to deliver us, when all the time he has already acted and done everything that is necessary, seems to me to be a gross neglect of an essential truth. We all agree that prayer is a good and a necessary thing, but when we are led to bypass the central truth of the gospel, I fear we have been greatly deceived.

We need to proclaim the truth that Jesus has overcome, and we need to come against all opposition using that truth. This is not magic, nor does it mean that God will do our will, but it does mean that we ask God to act using what his Son has already achieved.

Our task is to learn to live in Christ. Our constant temptation is to act outside Christ. Deep down in us is the drive to act on our own. We are *in Christ*, but if we act as though we were not in him, then we effectively act outside Christ. That is why Jesus said, 'Abide in me' (John 15:4).

Coping with temptation

Temptation, of course, will still attack us for we are not yet fully redeemed. When we sin we step out from the shelter where Christ has put us, exposing ourselves to evil. Temptation is to be dealt with, not by trying to resist with our own strength, but by putting it to death with the truth that, in Christ, we are dead to sin (as St Paul says in Romans 6). But what does it mean to be 'dead to sin'? I remember wrestling with this statement when I first began to pay attention to Romans 6. I would argue that I was not 'dead to sin' because I *did* sin. I began to realise that I did not actually believe this doctrine and so it was not surprising that I did not experience its effect in my life. It helped when someone told me that Scripture did not say that sin was dead to me, but that I, in Christ, was dead to sin. I started to see that I was being tempted to deny that I was in Christ and to follow the demands of temptation which I could feel very strongly.

Paul writes in Colossians, 'You must kill everything in you that belongs only to earthly life' (3:5). In another place he says, 'You cannot belong to Christ Jesus unless you crucify all self-indulgent passions and desires' (Gal. 5:24).

In practical terms this means learning to live in the fact that we are dead to sin in Christ, and when Satan attacks us, we retaliate with the truth that we are dead to this way of living and thus crucify the desires that are seeking our attention.

What we need to understand is that sacraments endure; they are not confined to the ceremony where they are administered. At baptism we both died and rose to new life in Christ and we are to live this truth throughout the whole of our lives. We must die to self every moment and rise to new life in Christ. To apply this truth to every rebellious thought is to put that thought to death with the truth.

When temptation attacks, our action must not be to try and resist in our own power, but to defend ourselves with the truth: 'I have died with Christ to that way of living. I have been bought with a great price and therefore I no longer have to submit as your slave. I belong to the Lord Jesus Christ.' Of course we do not use these exact words; to do so could verge on treating them as magic. It is our faith in what the Lord has done that saves us; how we express that faith does not matter.

Praying through the gospel message

We have seen that arriving at this place of conviction is not achieved by filling our heads with teaching and Scripture quotes as if they provide some sort of magic formula. That would be another subtle way of self-achieving. Only the Holy Spirit can lead us on to truth. He has to bring us to that place where we see and admit our inability.

This place cannot be reached by reasoning, study, will-power or asceticism. It comes to those who wait, to those who give time to prayer, who no longer wrestle to master everything; it comes to those who are content to live with mystery. Prayer, in its earlier stages, involves thinking – we wrestle with thoughts and questions. But later, as we begin to realise that no amount of thinking or reasoning can reach or capture God, we begin to let our heart be involved. I do not mean we sit still and just wait trying to think of nothing. That is not possible, and it could result in a very passive waiting.

I hesitate to say what I try to do when I pray for fear someone should think that they ought to do the same. We all pray in our own unique way and we should pray in the way we *can* pray and not in the way we cannot. I, myself, tend to think of Christ, either on the Cross or just risen from the tomb, but I try not to reason it all out. I resist asking questions about how it all happened, why it all happened – I just accept it as a fact. Then I endeavour to respond with gratitude, wonder and worship. This could take the form of words of thanksgiving or gratitude or just thoughts. I suppose I could call it a moment of adoration or worship. It is at such moments that I can get insights, or understandings, which are not like understandings that come after reasoning processes. It does not always happen at the time of prayer, sometimes it comes at odd moments when I am busy somewhere else. It is a gift and there seems to be a *knowing* without knowing how or why. I believe this is what revelation means.

The journey out of self into God is of necessity slow. We have to learn to get out of the driving seat and allow God to be the Lord and Master. That is not quickly learnt. There is no crash course. It comes to those who ask and wait. God has to get us to that place where we know for certain that we cannot live this life by our own decisions. This is not an easy journey, and Satan has a field-day taking truths and twisting them so that they seem ridiculous to us. For example: to be told that nothing we can do will achieve freedom from sin, makes us think that therefore we have nothing to do at all. That is not true. It is like growing seeds; we do not make the seeds grow, but if we do not sow and water them they will not grow. On the other hand to be told that we have something to do, can make us think we have everything to do.

Where is this teaching in Scripture and liturgy?

I suppose it is all too easy to imagine that because a person goes to church, has perhaps attended a

Catholic school, he or she has a clear grasp of the central teaching of the gospel. It is, however, quite wrong to assume this. Careful teaching is needed all our lives, for while we might have learnt much Catholic doctrine, we can be very ignorant about the essential truth of Christianity.

The teaching about being dead to sin in Christ is not at all easy to grasp and like so many difficult doctrines it can get left aside. I do not remember having any clear teaching on the subject, but that does not mean I received none. When something does not catch your interest or understanding, you often do not take it in even when it is mentioned.

After I had become aware of the teaching and began to see its importance, I noticed that the liturgy constantly referred to it. I am amazed how, in spite of this frequent reference, I had never before really noticed it. This shows how important teaching is, for if we have not firmly grasped that truth, it will be missed. How many times did I say the prayer at the end of the rosary, and never take in what I was really saying?

O God, who through the life, death and resurrection of your Son, has purchased for us the rewards of eternal salvation . . .

It states clearly here that salvation comes through the death and resurrection of Christ. The following texts all refer to this truth, although it has to be said that they do it rather obliquely, so it can easily be missed.

He is the Word through whom you made the

universe, the Saviour you sent to redeem us. (Euch. II Preface)

All life, all holiness comes from You through your Son, Jesus Christ, by the working of the Holy Spirit. (Euch. III)

. . . see the victim whose death has reconciled us to yourself. (Euch. III)

We offer you his body and blood, the acceptable sacrifice which brings salvation to the whole world. (Euch. IV)

Father in heaven, the love of your Son led him to accept the suffering of the Cross, that we might glory in new life. (Prayer for fifth Sunday of Lent)

Lord God, the Cross reveals the mystery of your love: a stumbling block indeed for unbelief, but the sign of your power and wisdom to us who believe. Teach us to contemplate your Son's glorious Passion that we may always believe and glory in his Cross. (Evening prayer, Wednesday, second week)

We have numerous teachings of Scripture that are saying the same truth, but in the past we Catholics have not been so good at reading our Scripture. Today things are greatly changed, and we can be much more aware of texts like:

For anyone who is in Christ, there is a new creation; the old creation has gone, and now the new one is here. It is all God's work. (2 Cor. 5:17–18)

We must realise that our former selves have been crucified with him to destroy this sinful body and to free us from the slavery of sin. (Rom. 6:6).

Paul goes on:

> When Christ died, he died, once for all, to sin,
> so his life now is life with God; and in that way,
> you too must consider yourselves to be dead to
> sin but alive for God in Christ Jesus. (6:10,11)

Here we are given instructions on how to deal with
the sin within us. We are to consider ourselves dead
to sin but alive *in* Christ Jesus. We are to fight using
this truth, and yet so few have been taught it. When
the gospel is not experienced as power, then it
becomes irrelevant and loses its bite.

We will not feel this new creation for we have
but the first fruits of it. Salvation has not yet been
completed in us, but it has begun because we are
one with Christ in our spirit. Life's journey consists
of allowing this new life to penetrate into our whole
being.

If you put a brick into water, you can say, 'the
brick is in the water', but is the water in the brick?
In time, because bricks are usually porous, the water
will seep in. At baptism, we were put into Christ,
and our journey through life consists in allowing
Christ to enter into the whole of us.

We need to pray for revelation so that we might
be given insight into this mystery of our life in
Christ. No human knowledge can achieve it – it
comes only to those who humbly seek it from God.

St Bonaventure clearly speaks of this truth in a
treatise 'On the Mind's Journey to God'. He says,

> We must set aside all discursive operations of the
> intellect and turn the very apex of our soul to God

78

to be entirely transformed in him. This is most mystical and secret. No one knows it but he who receives it. No one receives it but he who desires it. No one desires it but he who is deeply penetrated by the fire of the Holy Spirit, the fire Christ sent on earth. This is why the apostle says that this mystical wisdom is revealed through the Holy Spirit. If you want to understand how this happens, ask it of grace, not of learning; ask it of desire, not of understanding; ask it of earnest prayer not attentive reading; ask it of the betrothed, not of the teachers; ask it of God, not man; ask it of darkness, not radiance. (Reading from Feast of St Bonaventure)

8

Reconciliation Services

 As we have seen, Christ came preaching repentance and good news. He made peace by shedding his blood on the Cross, and he empowered his Church to minister that reconciliation continually throughout the ages.

We have seen how the early church progressed from thinking of baptism as the only sacrament that took sins away, to seeing the necessity for an ongoing sacrament.

Jesus empowered his apostles to forgive sins and they in turn empowered their successors to continue this work. The Church is Christ's continuing presence among us, even though it is made up of fallible humans. Together we form the Body of Christ.

When anyone commits a sin, not only is God offended but the Church is also offended because its presence and power in the world is made less effective. Therefore reconciliation is not to be sought only from God, but also from the Body of Christ here on earth. A priest represents the Church and when we confess to him we are confessing both to God and to the Body of Christ.

The Second Vatican Council decreed, 'The rite and formulas of penance are to be revived in such a way that they more clearly express the nature and effects of this sacrament.' From this decree came the New Rite. The Council also drew up a rite whereby several penitents can be reconciled, thus emphasising the communal aspect of the sacrament.

Of its nature this sacrament is private and the Church wishes to retain that aspect, and yet it also wishes to bring out the fact that we are all sinners and we all need to forgive each other. The new rite for public penance services guards the confidential aspect in that sins are confessed privately to a priest, and brings out the communal side by means of a penitential service held in common.

In such services prayers are said, and Scripture is read, since it is good for people to hear those texts that show the Lord's mercy and forgiveness. A homily is given and again this offers an opportunity for the love and mercy of God to be emphasised. To help people to prepare for the sacrament, the leader suggests areas of sin to be looked at and motives to be examined. This also affords a good opportunity for us to consider our joint responsibility for conditions in the world. A carefully prepared service can help people exercise a more mature examination of their lives. Also this sort of service can help a congregation get ready for the various Church festivals, thus enabling the group as a whole to participate in the feasts with a sense of having prepared together.

I have been at services where the priests are not

closed away but sit in a place where they can be seen. Seeing others at confession and receiving absolution can help us understand that we are all sinners and we all need this healing.

Permission whereby general absolution could be given was also granted at Vatican II, but since then it has been decided that it is up to the local bishop to grant such permission. Where this is not allowed, services have been devised to retain the confessing of sins to a priest, but the absolution is delayed until the end and is then given to all those who have confessed. This is another way of emphasising a sense of community.

Dealing with large congregations at these penitential services is not all that easy. A good number of priests is required, otherwise it takes a long time for confessions to be heard. Alas, these days it is not always easy to gather a good number of priests, especially in more rural areas. When there are few priests, it can become tedious for those who confessed early on and for those still waiting their turn. It is difficult to know how to occupy those not actually involved in making their confession to a priest.

The new rite has also provided for a celebration without absolution. This sort of service can be useful for often we need time to examine our lives, and it is only over a period of time that we begin to see what is happening to us. Ash Wednesday can be a suitable opportunity for such a service, for it sets the mood for Lent and begins a preparation for a deeper kind of confession.

As I have already mentioned, Vatican I (1869–70) had to be ended prematurely when it had only had time to deal with four of the fifteen points on its agenda. Those four points all had to do with the head of the Church. It is not surprising that the period after that Council was focused on Rome and Church leaders. Pope John XXIII saw that Vatican I had not been finished so he called another Council to complete it. That is why it was called Vatican II. In that Council the body of the Church was discussed. Since then the Church has been trying to make us all more aware of the fact that we are a body and our lives are not just our private affair.

The changes which have taken place are not just an updating. There was and is still a real need to make sure the central message of the gospel is clear. All changes are for this end. Teaching is very important and we live at a time when we could so easily try and be accommodating to everyone that we fail to teach the essentials to our children.

God has done wonderful things for us through his Son Jesus Christ. The Church exists to teach what he has done and to minister to its children his healing which he bought for us at such terrible cost.